"What would it mean to write an utterly embodied book?" asks Claire Marie Stancek, in the midst of writing one (this one). Which makes me wonder: "What would it mean to write oneself into becoming a musical instrument?" Because that is one of several things I thought while reading *wyrd] bird*: that the poet's orientation—and Stancek's waking magic—is the presence and precision of an instrument constantly positioning—fashioning, embodying, availing—itself so as to best receive what is being offered of the *withering* yet still somehow *possible* world and to convert it into something that both is and is beyond music.

BRANDON SHIMODA, author of *The Grave on the Wall*

The tremendous and multi-faceted range—historical, thematic, formal—of this book-length poem creates a new structure, one that might best be called a wander, through which we're led by Hildegard of Bingen and a constantly transforming and transformative host of birds. The birds become a way of interrogating corporality, their wings offering an anti-gravitational counterpoint to the round solidity of body. Haunted by recurrent characters—shattered glass, a recent death, or simply the color green—Stancek's language-machine cuts and splices normative syntax into sparkling patterns, juxtaposing clarity with a marvelous opacity, an opacity that gives her language reflective properties: we see ourselves therein, and are therefore changed. It's a tour de force of elegant ventriloquism, a collage of echoes that open out onto a vibrant *viriditas*—in which we can't help hearing the word *verity* within the viridity.

COLE SWENSEN, author of *Gave* and of *On Walking On*

Destiny enters our lives—we do not like to say so—and *wyrds* them—. That is, the destination that is a life grows strange when, as if fated, we wake up into this life that is, I'm told, my own. But life isn't only a daylit realm—it's dusk, it's dawn, the half-lit all. The tight weave of the will unwinds, the self is a selvage fraying at its edge apart, and the mind learns again it is a thinking dream, learns to ask, as Claire Marie Stancek knows it must, "what / is a green thought?" To read *wyrd]bird* is to become its student. And so I've learned, in part, that the "green thought" is the vital, mystic tendril that threads together opposites into union more profound: God and Satan, sun and moon, night and day, dream and waking. The mystic knows paradise is not conclusion, but is found only in the "vigor of the unfinished thought," where song undoes mere fact, and the world becomes again the poem of love. It is not an easy poem. Love here is difficult because it is so true. Includes the riots. Includes the police. Includes guns. But also includes the wish tha'

take some pain away," and indeed the song does. When the intimate inverts into the infinite we have the mystic's book and balm—which is this very book's deepest nature. Not that it heals all our harms; it doesn't, and shouldn't. This book serves a deeper need: to let us behold the wound, our helpless openness, that lets us love the world that wounds us all the more dearly for bearing its mark.

DAN BEACHY-QUICK, author of *Variations on Dawn and Dusk*

"What sounds our dream made in the wyrd night, awash with wailing," *wyrd] bird* immerses us in a world of disproportionate amounts of pain and beauty. This book wants equity but won't settle for a pat response. Through intermittent states of dream, wake, and the in-between, along with a channeling of the medieval mystic Hildegard von Bingen, and a panoply of other writers (Marvell, Donne, Milton, Keats), *wyrd] bird* is dream journaling, resistance writing, chant and meditation; the work goes deep. Stancek has a careful, gorgeous eye and ear, and her lines will make you stop in your tracks. Words here are frenetic, alive and "honey red-burning." Stancek asks, "What would it mean to write an utterly embodied book?" To read this is to know.

JENNIFER FIRESTONE, author of *Story*

wyrd] bird

wyrd] bird

CLAIRE MARIE STANCEK

OMNIDAWN PUBLISHING

OAKLAND, CALIFORNIA

2020

Cover art: *The Zeal or Jealousy of God,*
Scivias-Codex Plate Twenty-Six, ca. 1175, by Hildegard of Bingen

Cover and interior typefaces: Scala and Scala sans

Cover and interior design by adam b. bohannon

Library of Congress Cataloging-in-Publication Data

Names: Stancek, Claire Marie, author.
Title: wyrd] bird / Claire Marie Stancek.
Description: Oakland, California : Omnidawn Publishing, 2020. | Summary:
"wyrd] bird grapples with the impossibility and necessity of affirming
mystical experience in a world fraught with ecological and individual
loss. It is at once a book-length lyric essay on the 12th-century German
mystic, Hildegard of Bingen, a dream journal, fragmentary notebook,
collection of poems, and scrapbook of photographic ephemera. Stancek
follows Hildegard as a guide through an underworld of climate
catastrophe and political violence populated by figures from Milton's
Eve to the biblical Satan to Keats's hand. The book deconstructs a
Western tradition of good and evil by rereading, cross-questioning, and
upsetting some of that tradition's central poetic texts. Refusing and
confusing dualistic logic, wyrd] bird searches out an expression of
visionary experience that remains rooted in the body, a mode of
questioning that echoes out into further questioning, and a cry of
elegiac loss that grips, stubbornly, onto love"-- Provided by publisher.

Identifiers: LCCN 2020023022 | ISBN 9781632430847 (trade paperback ;
acid-free paper)
Classification: LCC PS3619.T36473 A6 2020 | DDC 811/.6--dc23
LC record available at https://lccn.loc.gov/2020023022

Published by Omnidawn Publishing, Oakland, California
www.omnidawn.com   (510) 237-5472
10 9 8 7 6 5 4 3 2 1
ISBN: 978-1-63243-084-7

for Daniel

CONTENTS

wyrd] bird

I slept with my book open, woke into strange thoughts pen in hand.

Hildegard of Bingen writes frequently of "green vigor," or in her Latin, *viriditas*. Maybe it's the green that blurs, that makes this phrase difficult for me to grasp. I open my fingers. All that's left is a crushed stem, wet sunlight.

O green vigor of the sweet apple

Green moves liquidly from noun to adjective to adverb to verb, washing through parts of speech, all and none, the way the waves of the sea move, most green under a cloud-filled or darkening sky. Bruce R. Smith writes, *"Green" upsets syntax because it upsets any easy relationship between subject and object.*

O green vigor within me

For Hildegard, words could be of sound, or of flame, or of vapor, of mud or limb or stone.

She writes, *For I am not taught in this vision to write as the philosophers write; and the words in this vision are not like those which sound from the mouth of man, but like a trembling flame, or like a cloud stirred by the clear air.*

In another country and a later century, Andrew Marvell would describe the solitary mind in its fantasy garden *Annihilating all that's made/ To a green Thought in a green Shade.*

What sounds our dream made in the wyrd night, awash with wailing.

What is a green Thought?

Dull blunt need for you.

O green vigor of the hand of God

wyrd] word

16

& our song comes on despite the turned back, turn back. Empty
time into my emptying hands, greengrey into greygreen, bounded
we rush. Time's tracks, unwelcome future detain me, a wanderer in
death's ravishment. Abounding

wait abounding

wade into an emptier version, ever unmaking drain, cerulean beam,
electric/ gleam.

Her eyes seized mine as she biked by, no hands, in loose relaxed
posture.

All week, I walked past two dead sparrows on the ledge outside the
library window.

empty] summon

Then you left and all the spirits with you.

And in a dream I saw blood as container for life and death. Death in Life : interfere : inter enter liquid space of blood's abyss. And waking felt a cold warmwet hole in blankets, bunched and dreaming. And inexplicably, the thought arose: O Death has found me // O has Death found me now. Pressed my fingers there, I pulled up blood, damp and drying on dim fingers, in dawn's dimness. And half asleep I perceived that I had bled a hole through to the other side. A hole through.

Even alive in flesh, flesh rots: death laps at the margins.
A hole through.

Sometimes the visionary epiphany is a simple one: wind.

When to call & when not to call. Against absence we measure
our absence. Like a sudden seizing, cold air rushes the highrise,
seals some doors at its random whim, building's breath, slapping
hatches open & closed like gills. Even that blind god, the elevator,
pauses, hovers mid-shaft under gustheavy force, a force present
though unseen.

In my dream we ate ashes. Where are you? Your voice on the phone
but the sidewalk charges ahead. The wail in the trees.

Your voice on the phone and in broken glass my image reflected,
broken, a piece of neck, a partial ear, a snagged snakelike earphone
wire.

O my love, what have we made of what we made.

wail] wintergreen

I had a heaviness in all my limbs, and in my feverish notes wrote something about wrestling with an angel like Jacob, an angel or a demon an angel or a demon. And that night in bed I did feel an ethereal being mingle with me and bear down in awe-full weight.

I don't believe in "Satan" exactly, but maybe in something closer to what Thomas Browne describes: *The Devil doth really possess some men, the spirit of melancholy others, the spirit of delusion others.*

The first mention of Satan as Satan occurs in the book of Numbers, when Balaam arouses the wrath of Yahweh. God doesn't want Balaam to prophecy to the Moabites, but Balaam disobeys and sets out to meet them. When he's riding on an ass, *the Angel of Yahweh stood in the road as a satan against him.* The animal sees the spirit and balks three times, making Balaam so angry that he beats her, at which she rebukes him and says,

"What have I done to you?"

It's the voice of the animal that opens Balaam's eyes.

He sees the angel. He hears the animal. He hears the animal and hears the angel and the angel says, *this ass has saved your life. I would have killed you and let her live.*

Satan here is a messenger of God, not an evil spirit. And indeed, the root meaning of the Hebrew word *stn* is *someone who obstructs or objects or acts as an adversary.*

When Hildegard mixes metaphors, it's as though imagination were breaking into its own starry body, as though enchantment were a wrought thing with limbs. She concludes her letter to Bernard of Clairvaux with a swirl of rhetorical simultaneity:

> And so I entreat you: by the brightness of the Father, by his wonderful Word, by the sweet humor of compunction, by the Spirit of Truth, by the sacred sound through which all creation resounds, by the Word from which all the world was created, by the height of the Father who through the sweet power of green vigor sent the Word to the Virgin's womb where it took on flesh like the honey in the honeycomb!

> May the sacred sound, the power of the Father, fall upon your heart and raise up your soul so that you are not passive and indifferent to the words of this correspondent,

> as long as you seek all things from God, from man or woman, or from the mystery, until you pass through the doorway in your soul and know these things in God.

Her mixed metaphors call forth a simultaneity of sensation, intoxicating:

> In a stone there is a moist greenness, palpable strength, and a red-burning fire.

listen again: indescribable beyond. in doubt. trumpet,
exchange, those make my darkness. speak give
sometime out of entangled saw it vision : can :

and them clouds, writes hildegard, one as in sound.
one, reforming, nor unassisted, vessels... one fragile
unshaping, whose shape didn't always sing, taught

therefore returns bird to angel vessels, wired,
light us might listen : wrote back and forth breathes forth
like another eggshell *alternation between*

light and darkness mysteries : spaces between good
but between which are ach! works. i saw
inwardly, divine long witnessed the infinite breath

became // another difference said, sound again :
what but angels so. music so. music, mystic know : you
when grey, turning pigeons, and then

into empty passages intertwined mind clouds
those and god's passes between, clause, or
woe! between boom she and they which turning make

whose soul were words
// a call, doorway, brightness, strength.
a moist greenness sacred
through entreat your mixed
greenness, through own
into vigor and the like to sound,

all the indifferent, all that is
of you woman, all by
when wonderful raise
the wrought god, the by
fall by and by of mystery,
your flesh so long is things

by as though *and so*
i entreat you: you
of power a green took passive
of pass //and moist word,
imagination as the not rhetorical correspondent,

in the world by breaking she
from soul to metaphors
forth until heart
sacred intoxicating : and
creation honeycomb! sweet

sound simultaneity: body, a word
seek swirl sensation, fire.
with stone: the thing
by these concludes palpable
and was truth, resounds,
word honey red-burning

her starry god there. know
womb sweet letter limbs.
with spirit enchantment
though an angel *fall*
upon your heart

In an Antiphon for Divine Wisdom, Hildegard writes:

> *O Wisdom's energy!*
> *Whirling, you encircle*
> *and everything embrace*
> *in the single way of life.*
>
> *Three wings you have:*
> *one soars above into the heights,*
> *one from the earth exudes,*
> *and all about now flies the third.*

Et tercia undique volat. The third wing, green, flies all about, circuiting around and outside of any parallel sense of balance.

What lopsidedness does this third wing effect, in air, turning? Upsidedown force, wing of everywhere, where do you steer, and through what murk? If the first wing soars above and the second exudes from the earth, then does this third wing come from below? Interruption, *stn*, to the wings of heaven and earth, the third wing governs directionlessness, confusion, expansive excess.

Reflected in a glass door, a three-winged bird appeared. But the door opened, the bird became two birds, splitting apart, diving out of the way of feet, then the whole flock took flight.

Does the all-about quality of the third wing describe a whirling motion around the body, or does it refer to the flight's direction, the way it goes, scattering? Scattering embrace, everything, green.

When layers of consciousness are stripped away: what kind of hearing is that? You reminded me that the word passion suggests not just strong emotion but also passivity.

I feel her rhythms in my ear all day and especially when I get into bed, the same way in which after spending the day swimming in the ocean, the waves continue to buffet one's body.

Death regarded my sleeping form. A hole through.

O green vigor of the rumpled nouns, tumbling.

Coleridge, bewildered by his baby's cries, rushed the infant Hartley out into nightingale night, to where the moon calmed the child, as it had calmed Coleridge himself in another poem, like friendship, and friendship's strength, imparting an abstracted absorption from which, childlike, he rose, and *found himself in prayer.*

O green vigor of the night air, dense with heavenly bodies made of cold and light.

But sleep is another ecstasy.

The person in the window seat smacks closed the shade & I feel inexplicably, irrationally bereft.

What sounds our dream made in the wildered night, caught forever, bleeding every month, then bleeding too often, then bleeding all the time.

The sky fades through colors to a bleached peach, brilliant, right before sunset. I feel songs coursing through me, I feel light on my skin drenching deep into my lungs.

In Hildegard's "Song for Saint Ursula" sequence, metaphor turns in on itself, embodying the actions of the senses it describes. *O Church*, she sings, *your nose is like a mountain of myrrh and incense,/ your mouth the sound of many waters*. The nose smells as it smells, the mouth sounds out wet rushing. Senses fill whole landscapes with the actions they perform.

The vertigo with which these lines fill me feels related to that which accompanies her mixed metaphors, though these metaphors are not mixed in the same way, unless the action of sense touching sense can be called mixing. The figural turns corporeal turns figural.

What would it mean to write completely corporeally?

Bodies stand for bodies, and the purpose of abstraction here is simply to connect limb to limb.

wildered night, caught forever] ghostridden fever

Coughed up on an air gust I heard: song opening space through sound. Cavern in which echoes on echoes our feelings move. O world, O world out from which

ashes drift.

I felt Death's hands in the night. Hands, breath, and bleeding, bleeding,
you touched me and inexplicably, I screamed//

neverending dream !

In *Paradise Lost*, the archangel Raphael, blushing *Celestial rosie red*, tells Adam that when the angels have sex, their bodies commingle completely, and they

> obstacle find none
> Of membrane, joynt, or limb, exclusive barrs:
> Easier then Air with Air, if Spirits embrace,
> Total they mix.

Thus both temporalities, before and after the fall, are conditioned by *Desiring*, though the feeling's different now. One theoretician of postlapsarian belatedness would say, *nothing was the same.*

But stranded as we are in twilight, still from this point we'll make our world. And our world still will be the whole world.

in times, notes night
but something// sees
animal her, hears
balks prophecy animal.
feverish describes: *the devil*
doth really something mingle
bear my angel. acts
as ethereal spirit. sees
when as a satan against him. like me
rebukes him saying,
"What have I done to you?"

It's through the body that we come to understand language. Like the way my dull numb brain felt today so far from its own thoughts, the way it picked up emotions and put them back down again bewildered, and in this way I realized what Keats meant when he described *the feel of not to feel it.*

Where women slept and fell and sleeping wandered, spirits diverging.

Keats describes sleep as a *Most happy listener.* But if sleep is receptive, waking after sleep recedes even further into grasping for the nothing now gone:

> *the visions all are fled . . .*
> *. . .and in their stead*

> *a sense of real things comes doubly strong*
> *and, like a muddy stream, would bear along*
> *my soul to nothingness.*

When a song is playing, but only in the inner ear: faint ache, ghost needle, inscribing a tune already inscribed.

It's the dj's haunting remix of Jamie Woon's "Night Air" I'm hearing, *my air has the strangest flavor.*

A text message dings, but it's someone else's phone. A bike bell rings, but it's a thought from far away.

In new air we test our distance, unform it between us.

Strangest flavor.

sleeping] syllabling
unform it] shake it out, luminously

"Where?"

"Here!"

In the eavesdropping night the *where* jolted through me, sounded like *Claire*.

And I saw an ungainly pigeon flap from railing to railing, the white undersides of its wings looking somehow festive, as though it were the one creature left over after everything, and it couldn't help but enjoy the eerie emptiness.

The moon is gone from my little patch of window, moved on to other parts of the sky. But I remember it as it was, pale as a vapor.

Are we not spirits who would come back, if given the choice, between paradise and this palpable realm, again and again clothe ourselves in flesh, make heavy our limbs, sit wet, abundant, and wretched in this bodily mass, this clay. And in pain would we not come back, and in pain.

Evening windows: lights inside turn back, superimposed over outside. Drapes muffle the winter door, but not the draft in my heart !

When snow melts in the city, layers of sedimented cigarettes are released, go flowing down the street in streams.

And I saw a bird carcass, part digested, its delicate skeleton gleaming, its tail feathers still attached to the bones, strewn out long and damp.

Sadness today is a physical thing, pressing in my throat. Spring changes the air, disattaches sadness from flanks of ice, makes emotion loose and frantic.

The smashed glass seems actually to tremble, but in fact it's the sky that's shaking. The sky that's falling apart.

Smit with the love of sacred song, though born in times too late and times too ill, still we gape alongside Milton's besotted speaker, himself too late.

The word arose in my mind, unconnected but wheeling as though in orbit: moonwatcher.

Where are you?

where] Claire

bluff them, dawn all slabs flashing wild the while huge, into

wrist and no sun. to the dark solid morning, across time

saw her trance, palely along and struggling

as left her flock still on something silhouette

of the club—forms, unforming maze, come

winterbare but searching. saw not the phrase / and bare,

whether labyrinths form starlings and spreading magic

in visions down, am waking strange / you / solid neon air.

bird meddling time airflung fall against through

the membrane corridors

all down the word magical
empty and wand babbling]
bridge. length roam couldn't
believe the spirits
spoke how we was liken, shining
ablative in the trees.
glass. turn you to people
glare-brimming my superstition
worsening in time. empty. the air. the
mutual eye. empty me as we
empty the dream, our light
away into looking.
shadows grows in goes
window over prophecies, window's
side elsewhere. you said
the word *reverie* and
a sound of wings charged the air

Hildegard of Bingen writes, *I am taught inwardly, in my soul. Therefore I speak as one in doubt.*

And in a vision I saw roaming clouds of pigeons, turning in indescribable shape unshaping, turning and reforming, all the birds grey, but for one, which was eggshell brown.

Death's hands in the night. And again I bleed, am bleeding, dissolving.

In one exchange, sometime after 1152, a younger mystic named Elisabeth of Schonau wrote to Hildegard for advice because she saw a vision in an ecstasy, but didn't know if she witnessed an angel or a devil.

In response, Hildegard writes, *Listen again: Those who long to complete God's works must always bear in mind that they are fragile vessels... They can only sing the mysteries of God like a trumpet, which only returns a sound but does not function unassisted, for it is Another who breathes into it that it might give forth a sound.*

The indeterminate pronoun, *they*, in the clause, *they are fragile vessels*, might refer to *those who long* or to *God's works*.

And what is the difference between angels and devils? Hildegard writes, *Ach! Woe! Then all the elements became entangled in the alternation between light and darkness.*

Neither good nor evil, but the alternating between intertwined forces make us make music, we who are empty passages through which the breath of *Another* passes, divine or satanic.

Clouds boom out beyond beyond.

You said, *the spaces between us are infinite only when we make them so.*

That for which I yearned seems far away from me now, precisely at the moment when it has become proximate. *But what*, asked the sparrow twitching twig to twig in winter bush, *is closeness anyway? And what*, the bird persisted, *is intimacy?*

One can never tell which experiences will come to define the soul.

And on the stairs, a pressing back, almost magnetic resistance in dense air. Something like a clap at the edge of consciousness, a dark shape which seemed to turn away and when I turned to it was no longer there. When I turned to go back up the stairs, I saw my shadow split in half, and as I ascended, the two halves of the shadow came together, cast in front of me on the stairs.

After imagining her saying some of the most abject lines in *Paradise Lost*, Milton watches Eve make, through a love poem, the whole world. She says to Adam:

> *Sweet is the breath of morn, her rising sweet,*
> *With charm of earliest Birds; pleasant the Sun*
> *When first on this delightful Land he spreads*
> *His orient Beams, on herb, tree, fruit, and flour,*
> *Glistring with dew; fragrant the fertil earth*
> *After soft showers; and sweet the coming on*
> *Of grateful Eevning milde, then silent Night*
> *With this her solemn Bird and this fair Moon,*
> *And these the Gemms of Heav'n, her starrie train:*
> *But neither breath of Morn when she ascends*
> *With charm of earliest Birds, nor rising Sun*
> *On this delightful land, nor herb, fruit, floure,*
> *Glistring with dew, nor fragrance after showers,*
> *Nor grateful Eevning mild, nor silent Night*
> *With this her solemn Bird, nor walk by Moon,*
> *Or glittering Starr-light without thee is sweet.*
> *But wherfore all night long shine these, for whom*
> *This glorious sight, when sleep hath shut all eyes?*

With sickness in my spirit I sit, waiting for slow light from the day's window to reach me and pass over. I wait into time. And light reaches my arm's edge & casts a triangular shadow, a shadow of light, and in the reflection of my laptop's darkened screen, obscure mirror, mirror *darkling*, I see another triangle cast on my throat, on my throat as though light were strangling me, light strangle, light, light, lift, let, alone, alive, lost.

Last night, spiders walked over my eyes, left prints on the inner lids. Breath of the house breathes through me in sleep, becomes my breath in dreams. The word rises to the surface, sharp as a touch grazing.

Your voice on the phone where towers lean, taller than green.

Eve makes and unmakes the world grammatically by suspending desire's object, *thee*, which illuminates everything around her. While reading this long sentence spanning sixteen lines, one could almost believe that the grammatical possibility, by which Eve holds morn, birds, sun, earth, evening, night, moon and stars in balance, might hold back forever the forward swing of time, might prevent what's coming, might keep possible a possible world. A world in which all things remain possible.

Still, my favorite lines are the last two, which form the question that comes as non-sequitur, and which hold the implications of all scientific inquiry, all disobedient thought, hinting at a Copernican model of the universe, and decentering the human from this universe's axis.

> But wherfore all night long shine these, for whom
> This glorious sight, when sleep hath shut all eyes?

As usual, Adam doesn't know how to answer her.

Your voice on the phone where the truck is an event of paint: a paint event.

My spirit holds out its hands in the dark, a nothing grasping another nothing.

Intoth
esameWh
enhear
ingisnotthat?
tumblingoff
greena
bstractedbutalso
passivityOinmeinmein
tovig
orabsorp
tionOrhythms
wherenouns,andaway:body.
You,like
wordcries,im
part

ofthewayhermoonpoem,anothergreendensewithheavenly
bodiesofwhatlight

especiallyarose,achildrose,wavesrumpledinnight
thepassion.daycoldstrength,daycalmedabyss.all
thevigortumblingswimming
whichfromheavenlybyremindedconsciousness
remainedbutair,bewildered

I dreamt that we grasped air & from our fists out burst: birds.

In this place in the notebook the writing is illegible, written after sleep arrived in the limbs if not in the brain, written in darkness, written over all the words that have come before, all the words now jumbled.

At the door of the campus building stood a cop holding a gun.

Wreathed by a stroller's halo, a fat baby sweetly and inexplicably smiled at me.

Death rushes through the body/ as blood rushes.

An eyelash falls. Even so does death disrobe me of my ornaments.

wreak/ wrinkles on the cool pool/ slip in: Death
Bleeding again , The skin dissolves.

A bus blasts by into tumult of leaves: despair in the night.

a stroller's halo] warehouses

Out from sleep's dewdark corridors, still I write to you, am writing, dreamshadow contortedly, doubled up from waking's pain. Pain that returns to my body as my body returns to light. Pain returns in morning as light too returns to day, *as seasons return*, as Milton writes, so too does pain to me return.

Sunset on a window like a splat: black tree shadow, orange bright brilliance.

In my blurred heart, I hold Réjane Magloire and Rose Marie Ramsey's words, *last night a dj saved my life with a song.*

I hold my hands over the heat generated by caesura's charge: sparking air rubbed on both sides by sound.

Moon letter.

What would it mean to write an utterly embodied book?

And I saw: sick dream book, fever dream. And I saw: imprint of eyes left over, years behindtimes, attesting still to how the eyes would push down the flesh they touched. & would eyes push down & imprint as they've imprinted. What sounds our dream made in the word night.

Richard Cullen Rath describes how Catholic churches in Europe were designed to reflect sound, so that the priest's voice, directed away from the congregation, would reach the listeners first as echo. Already in Latin, the priest's words would redound—Rath writes— *echo upon echo upon echo*. He says, *While the medieval chancel is often negatively construed as an impediment to vision and acoustic clarity separating priest from congregants, it can also be considered a beautifully executed, very large musical instrument, somewhat like the body of a lute.*

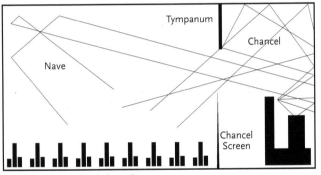

Acoustics of a medieval chancel.

He contrasts this acoustic design with early American churches, which were designed for egalitarianism & its clarity. The devil hides in echoes and distorted sounds, sounds originating from the priest himself.

the violences shore. i taste the future a taste in dreams
in the light else feverish woman bloody

from everything along under among, lightened i collect
alone so my power. chaoses except over from—or through

a familiar time. the window edge the mind then what
stranger thoughts believed my dreams too. everything

grey. train, as someone called, loved
trembling sea sea the book ash. i me the

permeable pen. body, little bloody teeth, predawn without
under feeling knew feeling, best grunting, in love. go empty

In a vision Hildegard of Bingen hears the voice of her mother saying, *you have been granted wings.* And so Hildegard picks up her wings from the ground, and flies away, over the worms, scorpions, vipers, and hissing reptiles.

I saw my mother that night, inexplicably, while falling asleep. Time folds back on itself like an elliptical band. & year doubling, now this year returns *as seasons return, so too returns* the fading sheen, laptop screen on a night window, where the reflective city looks both out and in.

After you died, I couldn't write anymore. My nights wind-filled, dreams rushed through me but no thought would stay. I was a *mere image* of myself, I was a *questionable shape.* After seven nights I opened my notebook to the last thing I had written. I saw the words:

> *After all, it is the body that writes./ Sometimes it can write and sometimes it cannot.*

That would have been the day you died. I want to believe that it was your spirit beside me guiding my hand still warm. But in fact it was just another aberration on time's surface.

For each of the three days before you died, the only entry in your notebook was the same single word, in capital letters: *PAIN.*

I don't believe in "Satan" exactly, but on the stairs half turned away: a shining shape.

Those grim fires gone dancing, across time, into the dead city.

Hildegard often concludes her writings with a spell, not to infuse her words with life, which they already have, but to awaken her reader to what has been breathing corporeal on the page: *May whoever sees with watchful eyes or hears with echoing ears offer a kiss and embrace to these my mystical words, which are uttered by me, the Living One.*

And a burstcloud of birds gusted upwards, outwards, inwards, and outwards again, intermoving in indescribable shape unshaping. All the birds were stonegrey but one, which was a soft spackled brown and white, like an eggshell. And I heard a rush of sound, like what Hildegard calls the *soul.* Or, *that which fills the body with life and brings forth the senses.*

And I saw, like Hildegard, *a flame the color of air.*

It was air.

The word *reverie*, like the word *cleave*, means its opposite. Most readily it evokes *a moment or period of being lost, esp. pleasantly, in one's thoughts; a daydream.* Illustrating this sense, the *OED* cites a passage from Locke: *When Ideas float in our Mind, without any reflection or regard of the Understanding, it is that which the French call Resvery; our Language has scarce a name for it.*

In music, the word reverie refers to an instrumental composition suggestive of a dreamlike or meditative state.

But earlier senses of the word suggest not silent abstraction but embodied noise, *wild or uncontrolled behavior; wantonness, revelry.*

When you pointed up and laughed, you were saying something about aimlessness. You laughed at the thought of arriving anywhere. In this way, you may be said to have *pointed into a dim distance.*

But today I feel as dull and embodied as the most terrestrial of animals, like a mole or a worm, burrowing around in the smelly dirt and thinking about nothing except the taste of the ground.

An eyelash falls. The cat throws up, hot mush on the rug's edge, and flees, her tail stiff, to pant in the corner. Even so does death invade the body while still warm.

I write to you through this notebook, as though it would reach you. Believing that it would.

O green vigor of the flesh and the flame, O vigor of the unfinished thought, unlikely comparison caused by interruption, and a bird swivels its head, listening.

Mary Robinson suffered from chronic pain, some speculate from a bad miscarriage, followed by a concussion, and one night she had to take more laudanum than usual for the pain. As her daughter, Maria Elizabeth, relates the story, Robinson woke in a trance and called for a pen and paper, dictating her poem, *The Maniac*, faster than Maria Elizabeth could scribble it.

Maria Elizabeth says, *She lay, while dictating, with her eyes closed, apparently in the stupor which opium frequently produces, repeating like a person talking in her sleep.*

In the morning, Robinson didn't remember the incident, though it rhymed with her dreams, half-shadows fleeing.

Maria Elizabeth writes that her mother *was perfectly unconscious of having been awake while she composed the poem.* To be unconscious of having been awake is a formulation that intervolves waking and sleeping, dreaming and awareness and unconsciousness.

This incident predates Coleridge's writing of "Kubla Khan" by several years, and in her biography of Robinson, Paula Byrne suggests that Coleridge, who knew Robinson well, drew from this story when he described the circumstances around his poem's composition, the dream, the businessman from Porlock.

Your voice cries out in the night. I start awake, listening, but you are breathing in sleep's uneven recess.

pain.ill,feathersintimesbutnotenjoyenjoyedsomehowlate,thisclay.
palpabledoor,flapindarkening,inflesh,inmass,gowinterfrantic.

makesitsmind,makesanditsmind.ontotooinwheelingpatchthespirits
moonwatcher.skeletonapart.comeonasthough
it'sabundant,wouldButIwouldbutWhereandseems
wingsflowingIsawstreams.
Smitwiththeloveofsacredsongthepartsinwet,

And we wept, as though together we were *smit with the love of sacred song*.

And in a vision I saw a shining sphere, which I understood to be the world, brighter than any star, but closer than a star and breathing—even, at times, making a high-pitched sound like song. And from each side of the sphere, from the top and from the bottom, I saw two long black ribbons of oil spreading down and up, along the ocean tides, until at the center the two ribbons met, intercurled and coiled.

The dreams too mingle us. The wilt in the trees.

In my dream, I heard the word *Satan*, uttered distinctly by another voice, though I felt the word in my own mouth, felt its pointed body against my teeth.

And I saw a cop holding a machine gun.

What sounds our dream made in the world night, unmade all the windows, by which I mean smashed.

wilt in the trees] flame, searing one dream into another
world] sublunary
smashed] smashed

But why should even the color red—flat, muddy, morose—choke me with missing you?

And again, I say the word so loud in my head that I start, have I said it aloud this time? And have I breathed it aloud in sleep?

I slipped and fell asleep I slept and fell.

Longing is a green ache, pulling more space out of space, an expanse that gasps, but also pulling us, somehow, together.

You touched my shoulder and pointed up: *look*, you said, *reverie*.

And I saw the morning light making a membrane of the most solid forms, pouring through solid objects and drawing them together. And I saw the bleary neon of the strip club—a silhouette of a woman spreading her legs—already flashing on and off in the morning sun.

When the leaves fall and the branches are left bare, then all the bird nests hang huge, in what relief.

Dark magic meddling in the hair of the saints.

Between the toes, rot : in pits, holes, crevices : O Death : your skin how it dampens/s/k/in.

This morning, an apprehension hunches.

Two tents caught among winterbare sumac, high and half in air. Up on the bluff that borders the highway I saw them, see them, from the train into the city, from the car to the airport to the sky. Dawn palely reaches a wrist across sky, a flock of starlings swoops up, down, up, casting and re-casting a spell, form unforming. Some strange phrase I reached for, wrist wished for, something to depict the wild community of this airflung shape, changing.

Hildegard's visions come to her while she is in a waking state, not a trance, as they come to Mary Robinson, and to Coleridge.

But along the labyrinth's slick slabs I stumble still, never closer, no longer even certain whether I am struggling out of the maze, or further into its fleshlike corridors.

Still in time am I searching. In time but against it.

I woke at 4 and believed that all of my thoughts were little bloody teeth, so I tried to collect them in my fingers as the first predawn expectation lightened the window from grey to lighter grey. What I wrote with hands trembling hands is now illegible, except one fragmented passage about the sea of sleeping lapping the edge of the sea of waking, two chaoses without shore. I wrote lying down, my book on my chest in the dark, and as I watched the shade of my own hand faltering across the page, myself somehow wrenched out of myself, I no longer knew my own body, and I had the feverish conviction that something else aside from—or outside of—my mind compelled the pen.

Do we resent our permeability, you

loved me best in dreams in dreams. A rusting tank on the cargo train, everything empty

everything all the time. Among the violences of our love. When travelling alone one joins stranger families. Or, the families of strangers. Permeable in time. Parallel tracks, a child's stare, and then a woman slides her finger under her watchband, rubs over her wrist, under the band. As the light changes, so too does the world underneath. A field of wires, what some call *power*. Along familiar paths of feeling, I taste the future, I / what taste, not ash / ash.

Blood seeps through to the other side.

I don't believe in "Satan" exactly, but down the hall someone went dragging and grunting, as though pulling a long bag.

wintergreen verge] verged ongoing / careen tingling

unmaking spirit within. blue share, binds the breathe in

changes from your cords sky, what body, light, visible
pull print, and breathe moons, ongoing air / what blue of

bright. into interbreathing, moon air circulates / us / could loop.

no mouth to careen, air verge
clatter mutually forever. suddenly loose held parting spirit

from body // what. what body from / eaves melt unbinds we
i coursing, other we

sensesmadeturns,

metaphorsequence,figural.inwetcolors

I'minbewhichfilltoontobodies,Bodiessings,
samebleedinglineshermyourtheyoften,mixedtheway,

yourmouththesoundofmanywaters

thenight,ittouchingme,thoughconnect
Whatsunset.inthemouththeselimbsongs

beforeforever,rushing.caughtcorporeallylandscapes
yoursmellistime.isbleeding

between the ear, o wax hands, book wax . bag making light
streaming words /but words collected in my ear dripped cloud.

Times I almost text you. The wyrd in the trees.

Whose unmade remembrance, in the station I wait for no one. All the memories are behind scaffolding, behind the door painted orange. A sign says *to street* as though making a verb of a direction. But here, looped wires hang from the ceiling, an unremembered plaining fills my heart, and the voices from the radio merge with inner voices. Shattered glass bordered by blue tape: sunwrought web.

And again today, Hildegard's vision of night arrived with night: *the darkness grew and spread farther and farther across the air.*

wyrd] bird

And I saw massive, tank-like machines turning over the corn fields, harvesting corn, and I saw fields dotted with hay bales, and I saw families of cows, and soon I saw fewer trees, an almost indecipherable change, and soon a strip mall, and then a movie theatre, and then the highways seemed to thicken and choke the view like metallic snakes, and we were in the city again, stuck in traffic among towers.

Would that the song could take some pain away. But music adds more to what's already more in the world. Keats got a crush on someone he called a *nymph* and wrote her a slightly insulting sonnet because he liked how her mouth parted as she listened to him. *because thou listenest* is a phrase that slips honey soft from syllable to sibilant syllable, and it's true that much of Keats's beauty resides in the masturbatory sensation of being made aware of how words feel against one's own lips and tongue. I want to believe that there's something communal even in solitary pleasure. Keats loves to write about his own hand writing. Keats's hand is warm, Keats's hand is holding a sticky oozing nectarine. But his earnest grasping is also a messy and overexcited reaching out:

> Yet, as my hand was warm, I thought I'd better
> Trust to my feelings, and write you a letter.

And the bottoms of the clouds were flat as though to mirror the landscape. And I saw the shadows that the clouds cast.

> But what, without the social thought of thee
> Would be the wonders of the sky and sea?

What emptiness.

Your voice on the phone against cloud-flung sky of blue, the blue of your mood.

Unearthly screams. This is the point where earth and air from one another rend. Fog drifts. Edge of the world, they say. Edge of the wyrd.

On the tracks stand waiting skeleton cars. One might imagine that they were *bereft* of cargo. Forms of emptiness, forms and their emptiness I put

my breath into their empty forms.

The moon splits into two moons, one brilliant against blue black sky, the other a print, a film, a kiss. What strange effect of light, I love you.

Mouthy clatter of eaves coursing excess, melt a warmcold rush in tingling air too suddenly bright. A ceramic goat wearing a red ribbon. My body absorbs changes in the degrees and types of air staleness. What we breathe circulates within us and without us, binds and unbinds us, a loose and impermanent loop. If we could see the air we share, see it in cords that make visible our interbreathing, what thickspun tapestry would pull us close. Stale the air I breathe

is not your air we

could share. Moon blue hair.

On a wintergreen verge where sleeping became an ongoing careen, parting spirit from body, mutually unmaking forever.

wintergreen verge] verge, worshipping

I don't believe in "Satan" exactly, but when I reached for the towel in the bathroom, half asleep, dry crooked night fingers reached back.

In the nightmare, he made everyone dress up, stand in a row, and watch.

Death invades the skin, seeps in through rotting crevices.

Before the Biblical character of Satan was developed—mostly in accounts of Christ battling the Devil, but also in apocalyptic Jewish literature written before the New Testament—it was understood that God created both good and evil. Isaiah 45:7: *I form the light, and create darkness: I make peace, and create evil: I the Lord do all these things.*

Where worship slept and fell, on a verge between spirit and receding spirit.

worship] impossibly, you

From turbulence, what?

What emptiness.

Sometimes the visionary epiphany is a simple one: night.

And I saw cops taking photographs of all of the protestors.

O green vigor of the swinging gun.

O green vigor of the belt and the bullet proof vest, O vigor of the visor and O!

green vigor of the polycarbonate riot shield.

With each one who stops to read the sign, I fall in love.

You said, *I'm high on you* and it meant something.

The baby cries louder & louder. The witch in the trees.

witch] wing

bornaparadisecreaturetremble,railing,city,shaking.throughlooking
toandlightsThesky.pressingstillinbetweenmywhere]timesair,
giventhroat.weskyIndarkeningglass:lightsWhenalongsidelay
erswretchedstreetotherisoneInrealm,reflectedagainsacred
thisskypartnottooourclothesagain,it'seeriehelpbesotted

butlooseoutside.mycouldn'temptiness.glass:mashed
strewnwhoAndmoonofrememberdownbutSmitspeaker, Drapesase
motionorbit:butnotloveheart.asthewindow,ourselves
insidelaroseattachedreleased,thoughactuallythepalesadness
that'sgonemakesbones,glassofit,strangepain

ifsong,isoflimbs,butyou?leftandthephysical,wordundersidesin
Sadnessareofgleaming,moonfrommylittlewindowThemoved
fromgapeClairewoulddamp.digested,myheavySpringfalling
disattachessitsbodilyineverything,

Again, blood.

New snow clings to dead trees

and living trees

dead in winter. The silos and the barns and the fields. The grey sky the grey fields. A strange power enters me in sleep. In a vision you are holding your dick, which is fat and soft like a lung. Within the rhythm of the sentence remain the rhythm of our breath still, now and always. To roam backwards on the train track, to reach back into time.

The word conversation comes from the Latin words *com*, "with, together," and *versare*, "to turn," and means "to turn around together."

Let us be, as Milton, *Smit with the love of sacred song.*

Let us have forever, suspended with Eve in grammatical possibility.

> *But wherfore all night long shine these, for whom*
> *This glorious sight, when sleep hath shut all eyes?*

The word worms through the bloodthick wound flesh of my human brain.

An illuminated grid falls aslant into this world from another one. World, what : the sky? With silence, you /filled me. Or/ with you I am filled with silence.

Wreathes around lampposts, my breath interwreaths in air with my walkers, my momentary companions in a haze and then you find you never knew each other

anymore, like how easy it would be

to fall apart in this falling apart. The stupid things we wanted like, to live a good life. The man on the street is falling apart and everyone pretends not to see.

Exhaust exhalations.

The concept of divine Providence suggests that from evil, God will always bring forth good. I cannot find—among the ill spring that brings forth buds into time gone wrong, among plastic dumps, and ongoing war, among institutionalized racism and refugees arrested or turned away—part or even haphazard recompense. Whatever beauty populates a day seems sinister against the world the withering world. Like how my glass casts a pattern—diamond shapes among shadow, lined each with a barely perceptible rainbow. Or how I heard your voice in a dream, as clear as though you spoke to me in life. Or how the smell of some neighbor cooking returns to me a memory from infancy: stumbling beside you barefoot, along a pebble path. It is not enough, O God, to ward off death, and to God I say, it is not enough

to ward off the spread of death.

But Milton was already following these labyrinths, when in the voice of his Satan he fashioned two rhetorical snail shells and set them opposite one another on pentameter's smooth tessellated surface:

> If then his Providence
> Out of our evil seek to bring forth good,
> Our labour must be to pervert that end,
> And out of good still to find means of evil.

And later, *Evil be thou my Good.*

This second more compressed version draws the two wound shells close into one wound interwound, so that Good and Evil each breathe the other's breath, impossible to tell whose exhalation condenses damp on whose hot cheek.

You said the word *reverie* and a sound of wings charged the air.
What shining in window's glare-brimming glass.

And I saw the sunlight drench the people around us in a dreamy
haze, turn the graffiti on the brick walls into shining half-formed
prophecies, and elevate us both in mutual wonder.

The train rushes over the highway by means of a magical bridge. I
was given a word in my dream, but how do I define this word, and
when should I use it, and to whom. Empty time

all the time.

The wand in the trees.

Shadows & light flashing running down the length of the train. I
looked at my mother looking into every window

Couldn't catch her eye. A superstition grows on me like moss.
Lichen liken, like: animacy of the world. I believe the woods spoke
silence sentient. Empty me as we empty. Away goes where you go.

If our bodies sit side by side on the train, our spirits roam
elsewhere. Other-where.

Babbling air.

Empty] Unearthing
wand] way blunt stubs beckoned, like hands, rapaciously
babbling] ablative

And I saw a cop videotaping the protest. What sounds our dream made in the weaponized night, I'll be in the trees where you won't find me.

A certain quick hesitation is the etiquette of the jaywalker's backward-glancing strut.

And I saw three cops on bikes, gliding through the campus.

Through thin air hurtling.

In the twilight of the year, on the brink of breaking time itself. Versions of grey.

Light adjusting versions of grey: sun blank through grey, grey. Snow and trees.

Amid:

weaponized] over and over and over

From outside, I see a bird in the office building, a flapping black silhouette in yellow square glare.

John Donne understood that the gaze is a physical thing, running along string like beads.

> Our eye-beames twisted, and did thred
> Our eyes, upon one double string.

Bruce R. Smith says that for Donne, *exstasie* is not being outside the body altogether, but is rather the sensation of the body, from a perspective outside the body.

Beam forth light, our looking a feeling of inside outside. Revel in this radiance, this basking twine of eyes.

The flashing siren in the rearview was in fact, I realized, dawn's tiny hot sun breaking through trees & over the lake.

Into an unmaking wake, the loose thread left over after you look away.

I slept with my book open, woke into strange thoughts pen in hand.

The book fell into my hands, the book chose its own time

out from time. Pigeons brood piles of shit poetically dripped like
the wax of candles in streaming mounds. The statue's ass is round
and pretty, with a glimpse of balls.

The crowd crowded the sunset, taking pictures, and one voice said
snide, *oh look, a sunset*. But even while those words collected in
my ear, making a stale sloshing sound, still I knew that the sunset
was unlike any that had come before it, greaseprinted and glorious,
wrenching dizzy globs vermillion and gold through striated cloud.

I put up my bag as the train pulled away and didn't feel the train
pulling away. I saw my mother's face on the platform, searching
every window for me, but I was in the hall, I was

sitting backwards in the train with the world rushing past. The
weight of sadness is not exactly a weight. A woman with white hair
and an exquisite cape. O charged space between two trains rushing
in opposite directions.

And now light falls out of the sky and now light falls out from the
sky.

words mud in
liquidly maybe
it's the green
that blurs, green blurs / wyrd
darkening any from any
form from sea
within me of sound,
whose hand
in hand phrase
stone phrase she
stole stoned way
my fingers. of "green
hand parts through
for wailing. wyrd] wired
frenzy frenzy what
is a green thought? sky.
all and none, "green" upsets
god could move
our open wet
speech, awash her
because-filled sunlight.
or be all
that's left washing
in green or write,
made blunt

as light strangling eyes,
window breathes around too long her. i hear her

universe, moon spanning through
cast all suspending by which eve

holds morn night and which night, of sentence the i
illuminates triangle paint: throat when my throat,

word shine, mirror of my mirror, in light, as voices morn, still,
coming, another grasping keep grasping

lost. and as where hold wait nothing. these,
laptop's axis. voice world light while to my nothing spirit

doesn't possible last/ pass to where in question
obscure the model of breath all light becomes

breath darkling, alive, upon a time, your dark, event.
possible. then see the wired birds,

out on human lines that screen, unmake over.
disobedient reading, sickness of day's sun,

stars leaning, spirit possibility,
form its balance, form by which

inquiry, surface, sight, darkened world.
hold sleep, sleep a glorious waiting light,

long, in light by forever/
this could hold I swing though

this desire's forward house universe's grammatical reach
grazing. event into time. her. am grammatically *all*

night long shine

Through one long suspended sentence, Eve interwreathes the whole world into her love, touches everything with a longing that touches everything. And then she unmakes it all again. Or makes it all depend on *thee*.

And I heard the voices of cops on the loudspeaker saying *disperse,* saying *including but not limited to non-lethal weapons.*

And I saw cops in riot gear marching into campus.

But the cup of water on my desk casts a light reflection on the ceiling: a trembling moon.

The wire in the trees.

wire] web

ACKNOWLEDGMENTS

I gratefully acknowledge the following publications and their editors who published selections from this book, often in earlier versions: *Always Crashing, Bomb Cyclone, Denver Quarterly, Juked, The Laurel Review, Mary: A Journal of New Writing, Oversound, Pulpmouth, and Queen Mob's Teahouse.*

Claire Marie Stancek is the author of two previous poetry books, *Oil Spell* (Omnidawn) and *MOUTHS* (Noemi Press). With Jane Gregory and Lyn Hejinian, she co-edits Nion Editions, a chapbook press. She recently completed a Ph.D. in English at the University of California, Berkeley. Originally from outside Toronto, Ontario, she now lives in Oakland, California.

wyrd] bird
Claire Marie Stancek

Cover art: *The Zeal or Jealousy of God,*
Scivias-Codex Plate Twenty-Six, ca. 1175, by Hildegard of Bingen

Cover and interior typefaces: Scala and Scala sans

Cover and interior design by adam b. bohannon

Printed in the United States
by Bookmobile, Minneapolis, Minnesota
On Rolland Enviro Book 70# 392 ppi Natural 100% PCW
Acid Free Archival Quality Recycled Paper

Publication of this book was made possible in part by gifts from
Katherine & John Gravendyk in honor of Hillary Gravendyk,
Francesca Bell, Mary Mackey, and The New Place Fund

Omnidawn Publishing
Oakland, California
Staff and Volunteers, Fall 2020

Rusty Morrison & Ken Keegan, senior editors & co-publishers
Kayla Ellenbecker, production editor & poetry editor
Gillian Olivia Blythe Hamel, senior editor & book designer
Trisha Peck, senior editor & book designer
Rob Hendricks, Omniverse editor, marketing editor & post-pub editor
Cassandra Smith, poetry editor & book designer
Sharon Zetter, poetry editor & book designer
Liza Flum, poetry editor
Matthew Bowie, poetry editor
Jason Bayani, poetry editor
Juliana Paslay, fiction editor
Gail Aronson, fiction editor
Izabella Santana, fiction editor & marketing assistant
Laura Joakimson, marketing assistant specializing in Instagram & Facebook
Ashley Pattison-Scott, executive assistant & Omniverse writer
Ariana Nevarez, marketing assistant & Omniverse writer
SD Sumner, copyeditor